A Course in
FORGIVENESS

Meditations That Release Suffering
To Bring Peace and Wholeness

BOBBI STOBBART-KASZA

A Course in Forgiveness
Copyright © 2019 by Ramona "Bobbi" Stobbart-Kasza

All rights reserved. No part of this publication may be reproduced, distributed, or transmitted in any form or by any means, including photocopying, recording, or other electronic or mechanical methods, without the prior written permission of the author, except in the case of brief quotations embodied in critical reviews and certain other non-commercial uses permitted by copyright law.

Tellwell Talent
www.tellwell.ca

ISBN
978-0-2288-1628-7 (Hardcover)
978-0-2288-1626-3 (Paperback)
978-0-2288-1627-0 (eBook)

Table of Contents

Dedication vii
Acknowledgements... ix
Glossary of Terms used in A Course in Forgiveness xi
Author's Note xv

Part One: Introduction... 1
Part Two: Forgiving Safely 5
Part Three: A Course in Forgiveness............................... 7

    Meditation 1... 8
    Meditation 2... 10
    Meditation 3... 12
    Meditation 4... 14
    Meditation 5... 16
    Meditation 6... 18
    Meditation 7... 20
    Meditation 8... 22
    Meditation 9... 24
    Meditation 10... 26
    Meditation 11... 28
    Meditation 12... 30
    Meditation 13... 32
    Meditation 14... 34
    Meditation 15... 36
    Meditation 16... 38

    Meditation 17 40
    Meditation 18 42
    Meditation 19 44
    Meditation 20 46
    Meditation 21 48

Experiencing Unconditional Love 50

Part Four: Forgiveness As A Spiritual Practice 52
Part Five: Reflections For Forgiveness As A
    Spiritual Practice 56
Part Six: Where To Go From Here: Taking A
    Forgiveness Walk 63
Part Seven: Epilogue 67
Part Eight: Addendum 68
Part Nine: Works That Inspired A Course in Forgiveness ... 72

Ramona "Bobbi" Stobbart-Kasza 76

"The Most Important step out of the karmic law is forgiveness."

Eckhart Tolle

Dedication

For Leslie and Sebastian,
who join me in my forgiveness walks every day.

Acknowledgements

First and foremost, I would like to thank my beloved husband, Leslie, who believed in me and in my message; he made my journey with this book possible through his hard work and support.

And my son, Sebastian, for bringing me to my knees with forgiveness for myself as a parent, and as a friend. He truly inspires me to be the best I can be and to follow my passion by leading by example and by living with that same dedication in his own life's journey.

I am so grateful to Eckhart Tolle for the inspiration I found through his books, specifically, *The Power of Now*, and *A New Earth*, and to Oprah Winfrey, for sharing Tolle's work through her dedication to healing and love.

And thank you to Richard Gerber M.D. and Deepak Chopra M.D., whose work showed me that health professionals can share important healing information founded in science and also in spirituality and ancient teachings.

My thanks must go to my dearest friend, Wendy Pawliuk, who stood by me when I doubted myself about writing *A Course in Forgiveness*. Wendy, too, leads by example, as she walks her forgiveness journey with such amazing courage and truth; she constantly guides me back onto my path.

Thanks to Shelagh Kennedy for working with me to learn how to be brave about putting this message and my truth out to the world. She has helped me to have confidence and courage to embark on this adventure.

Thank you to Lynda Goodman of Wellness Ink for her coaching, and thanks also to Bill Kachman, my lawyer and friend, for helping me to see all the important issues before I jumped in, and for forgiving me when I change my mind.

I am so grateful to my editor, Dr. Carly Kenny (Cape Education Services). I am grateful for her patience and her incredible talent; I am so glad that I knew that I needed an editor and found Carly. When I got stuck at times, Carly helped me with words and the expression of ideas that remained true to the soul of this message – she is truly a great writer.

And last but not least, I wish to thank my family, friends, and the Source, to whom I am indebted for my greatest lessons in forgiveness: without our journey together, I would not have been able to write this book.

Glossary of Terms used in A Course in Forgiveness

A Course in Forgiveness is a journey, and as such, it has words that describe ideas that point to possibilities.

The glossary that follows is intended to broadly describe what some of these words mean, in the context of this course. These are the words and explanations that I usually use with my clients. I had to innovate some of the concepts, as I could not find other ideas to represent what I meant to say when talking about forgiveness in terms of what I consider a spiritual energetic model. I coined terms like *Being-Consciousness* and *Ego-Consciousness* to describe ideas of how consciousness may be manifesting itself in us.

1. Forgiving: An action; a spiritual practice in which we make a choice to release any ideas or actions that we sense are affecting our peace and energetic wholeness as a Being.
2. Being: Has at least two manifestations, our solid form, in which we manifest on this earth (commonly called a *Human Being*), and a formless spiritual manifestation, an energetic Being connected to a Higher Power of our Understanding. All life-forms

in creation are energetic Beings in either the form or the formless sense.
3. Spiritual: A manifestation in consciousness of all of creation that, paradoxically, defies definition.
4. Duality: The idea that we are separate from all of creation to any degree.
5. Non-Duality: The idea that we are irrevocably connected to all creation and the source of creation. How it is named does not change the source.
6. Being-Consciousness: A consciousness that operates unattached from, but part of, form. It has no judgement or resistance to what IS. It exists within Ego-Consciousness in the experience of what we call *my life*. Its environment is the Eternal Now.
7. Ego-Consciousness: A consciousness that operates to create form by the way of things, ideas and concepts in its existential construct of *time*. These operations of consciousness enable us to experience what we call *my life*.
8. Mind-based *time*: An existential construct that Ego-Consciousness uses to mark the passage of events in the linear direction of past, present and future. While it does not truly exist, the construct of time is useful for us to plan our lives as forms, but it can confuse us in our experience of the Eternal Now. Ancients have referred to Mind-based *time* as the *Maya*, *Illusion* or *Veil* to true existence.
9. The Eternal Now: A term use by ancients to describe the only true state of existence – all that exists can only exist, right NOW - existence beyond the *Veil*.

10. A Higher Power of Our Understanding: A phrase that may represent anything from an idea of the Divine, God, Nature, a group or any concept or entity that inspires deep, often undefinable, meaning for an individual about their existence. Ultimately, this is personal, specific and meaningful to the individual or group.
11. Divinity: For the purposes of this book, Divinity represents a concept of a non-dualistic spiritual state; being at one with the Higher Power of Our Understanding - our wholeness as *Holiness*. The reader may substitute any concept that is meaningful to them.
12. Holiness: For the purposes of this book, Holiness is literally the wholeness of your spirit form. IT is always present as an inseparable connection to whatever you identify as the Source of all creation, or a Higher Power of your understanding. Your Divinity is within this spiritual wholeness; it is an expression of IT. It is you as IT, rather than IT as separate from you (Non-Duality).

I do not consider myself an academic authority in anything; I am just a traveler in my own creation story that I write as *my life*.

It is vital when reading *A Course in Forgiveness* to understand that concepts which describe others and creation as being separate from us (dualism) can be limiting, with regard to awakening the knowing of our Divinity.

A Course in Forgiveness also demonstrates a paradox when stating that we are the most important factor in the choice to forgive, but it is our connection to ALL (non-dualism) that makes the miracles inherent in forgiveness a reality.

I deliberately chose to parallel the name of this book with the 1970's book *A Course in Miracles,* by Helen Schucman, because this too points to our Divinity, the power of forgiveness, non-duality, the Eternal Now, and the illusion of time as its main themes. Both books teach that forgiving is a miracle that we can perform to heal ourselves and all of creation. Schucman shares, through inner dictation, her re-interpretation of Christian scripture and exercises emphasizing non-duality; in my offering, I deliberate extrapolations about non-duality, spirituality and consciousness through energy healing, quantum mechanics, and other overlapping sciences at a very simple and mysterious level.

It is my hope that *A Course in Forgiveness* will add the practice of forgiving as a spiritual action to your life, so that you may experience wholeness and peace.

We are all the manifestation of consciousness, as creation.

Enjoy your journey!

Author's Note

A Course in Forgiveness was originally written for all those like-minded people who embrace an energy-based body/mind paradigm toward their wellness and wellbeing. However, as I was writing this book, it became apparent to me that it could be beneficial to anyone seeking relief from suffering.

This book is my common-sense solution to repeating myself about the power of forgiveness to heal us and the answer to the question, "Why don't you just write a book about it?"

As I experienced the miracle of what forgiveness could do in my own life, and saw it similarly in patients, I knew that I had to relate this to others. I searched for books on the subject, but I found nothing which focused on a body/mind energy model, nor one that dared to speak to our Divinity - our wholeness with all of creation, or our *Holiness*.

I then tried to write *A Course in Forgiveness* in logical chapters with catchy titles, many times. But failed. I think I wrote this book over and over about four times, seeking to add more and more content.

The wall which I kept encountering was that so many know that forgiveness is *a good thing to do*, but so few feel that they would be able to do it: this, I was not interested in writing about.

This conundrum of how something so good could be so readily avoided intrigued me. "What was missing from the equation?" I would ask myself. "How could this powerful miracle of life be so missed by so many, especially if it is so beneficial?" Then, an answer finally came to me.

One day, after two years of attempting to write, I sat at my computer, on the point of surrendering to my failure, ready to just give up, I exhaled and sat quietly, listening within. Suddenly, and with ease, *A Course in Forgiveness* meditations that you will see in this book just flowed from my heart and mind, through my fingers to the keyboard, within a very brief amount of time. After about 20 minutes only, though I did not sense time passing as I typed, I had found and expressed my message. When the keyboarding stopped, I knew the book was done. Some might call that channeling; I call it a miracle - an event in the Eternal Now.

Later, try as I might to edit the meditations (outside of typos), it just would not come. It seemed that the meditations just wanted to stand as you see them now, despite my ego-consciousness wanting to add more content or change things, while I muttered to myself, "they will think I am crazy!" (More about ego-consciousness later.) All I have added to *A Course in Forgiveness* meditations is this author's note, the introduction, a glossary of terms, a few short chapters with practical ideas, and references to the literature I read while devising this book.

I make no attempt at trying to tell anyone what *A Course in Forgiveness* meditations mean, they are to be experienced on a personal level, by those who wish to do so.

So, try to imagine me just sitting with you, smiling and waving my hands with excitement and joy, as I work with you and support you lovingly through this exploration of the power of forgiveness to heal your life.

Know that I was just as surprised as you may be about what this book is suggesting, evoking our Divinity to be whole (Holy) and have peace. And most of all, I am grateful that I too can focus on my forgiveness work as a spiritual practice, just as much as anyone else.

It is not my intention to try to alienate anyone from their beliefs. This book is just an invitation to consider forgiveness in a new way: as a spiritual practice that can lead to healing, rather than a religious exercise. All readers, no matter your personal beliefs, are, of course, free to be curious, enlightened, confused, or even outraged by what I have written here.

When all is said and done, *A Course in Forgiveness* is what I believe I came into this incarnation with all of creation to write. The book has within it the possibility of recalling our Divinity through the experiences in our own life stories.

> *"I know that forgiving myself and others for errors of the past, heals ME."*[1]

Candice Pert Ph.D.

Go with peace and love
Bobbi Stobbart-Kasza

****

---

[1] Pert, Candice B. (2007). To Feel Go(o)d: The Science and Spirit of Bliss. Audio CD. Soundstrue.com

PART ONE

Introduction

Many people during their lives discover that, no matter what they do, they cannot find peace or a sense of deep meaning for their lives. Many also have vague or major illnesses that seem to have taken them hostage; they simply feel as though they are "just waiting" in the passage of their lives.

From my perspective, both now and in my previous nursing career in a critical care unit, I sense and discuss how grief, regret and loss can continuously weave through our lives. The source of grief can be from the loss of a loved one; the source of regret and anger can be from the harm done to us by others or by ourselves. These are obviously deeply personal experiences, which have powerful impacts on our wellbeing.

I am now retired from working as a Registered Nurse and Occupational Health Nurse and focus all my efforts on Bioenergetic Spiritual Healing. In this role, whenever I encounter situations that are besieged with grief and regret, with profound respect and gentleness, I invariably bring up the idea of forgiveness. I simply seek to discover if forgiveness has a place with my clients in their current circumstances. I often sense that unfinished forgiveness plays a part in their suffering.

In my experience, many of my clients have been shocked and even indignant by the idea of forgiveness, but when broached, so often, and within minutes of seeing their own wound of despair, they would weep.

Later, they would tell me that they did indeed hold "oceans of anger and resentment," at people or situations that they felt, to any extent, to have caused their suffering. They also lamented that they could not fully reconcile with forgiving, saying, "I can forgive (maybe), but I will never forget!"

With time, some would move toward forgiving; others would not. I had no attachment to the outcome either way, as the process in which they dealt with their sufferings was truly their own, but I did marvel at how those who forgave, would change.

Those who could see their way to releasing the story of their pain (and forgiving), would return to my office with more colour in their faces, smiles shown in their eyes, and new lightness of being in their lives. To me, those who forgave, seemed able to begin to participate in their own lives again. Often, they told me that, once they decided and acted on forgiving, they almost immediately felt the pain of grief and rage again of what had harmed them and/or others originally, but then (as I paraphrase their feedback), they moved into a sense of peace where they knew that changes were happening and new possibilities were ahead of them.

It was so evident to me that something definitely happened when they forgave: something powerful. From my knowing about what forgiveness does to us, I believe that in forgiving, they had remembered their Divinity, and with this, they experienced wholeness and peace in their lives. From here, they could participate in their own lives again to create new meaning.

"You are the universe expressing itself as a Human Being for a little while."

Eckhart Tolle

PART TWO

Forgiving Safely

Ideas we can use to forgive in a manner that creates safety for us and for others.

1. Forgiving never makes the harm done to us or others acceptable, explainable or excusable, unless we choose to deem it so.
2. Boundaries are always OK. Recalling the Divine in us does not mean that we must place ourselves or others at risk of harm in order to forgive.
3. We need never have a direct encounter with perpetrators of harm.
4. Forgiving is not time sensitive: we forgive when it is right for us, and for us alone.
5. When we forgive, we do not require any acknowledgement or co-operation from those who have harmed us.
6. Forgiving may be done silently within us, with or without recognition of the support of A Higher Power of Our Understanding.

7. Forgiving may be done as a choice to forgive and then as the act of forgiving.
8. Forgiveness is the way that you release yourself from pain and suffering: forgiving frees you, brings you to your wholeness and permits you to experience peace.

PART THREE

A Course in Forgiveness

Forgiving Is The Release That Makes
Us Whole (Holy) Once More

***Clear your mind;
relax your breathing – slow and calm;
open yourself to inspiration.***

Bobbi Stobbart-Kasza

Meditation 1

You are, and have always been, an Eternal Divine formless Being.

You are now having an earthly experience in your solid form called a Human Being.

You exist only in the Eternal Now, where cycles of change in energy from the formless to form are the basis of all creation.

You have temporarily forgotten this truth.

- Awaken.
- All of creation is ONE, Divine and Eternal.
- Forgive yourself. Forgive others. Forgive everything. Remember your Divinity and end your suffering.

Meditation 2

You are, and have always been, an Eternal Divine formless Being.

You are now having an earthly experience in your solid form called a Human Being.

You exist only in the Eternal Now, where cycles of change in energy from the formless to form are the basis of all creation.

You have temporarily forgotten this truth.

As an Eternal Divine Being, you are inseparable from all that exists because you are IT, and IT *is* you.

This singularity happens because you arise from the formless that is the Source of all creation.
The Source is a state of pure potential and unconditional love. What you name it is only relevant to you, but it can never change what IT is.

- Awaken.
- All of creation is ONE, Divine and Eternal.
- Forgive yourself. Forgive others. Forgive everything. Remember your Divinity and end your suffering.

Meditation 3

You are, and have always been, an Eternal Divine formless Being.

You are now having an earthly experience in your solid form called a Human Being.

You exist only in the Eternal Now, where cycles of change in energy from the formless to form are the basis of all creation.

You have temporarily forgotten this truth.

EVERYTHING is Divine, because all arises from the Source: all experiences, all things, all ideas, and all of creation.

Your Being-Consciousness knows that there are no mistakes; there are just opportunities to evolve your own consciousness.

- Awaken.
- All of creation is ONE, Divine and Eternal.
- Forgive yourself. Forgive others. Forgive everything. Remember your Divinity and end your suffering.

Meditation 4

You are, and have always been, an Eternal Divine formless Being.

You are now having an earthly experience in your solid form called a Human Being.

You exist only in the Eternal Now, where cycles of change in energy from the formless to form are the basis of all creation.

You have temporarily forgotten this truth.

You use consciousness to operate your Human Being form: A Being-Consciousness and an Ego-Consciousness that you express as a dance of expansion and contraction in your own creation of *time*.

Being-Consciousness awakens in you and leads you to the truth of your Eternal, Divine Nature; what is real in you.

Ego-Consciousness creates situations in your mind that cause you to temporarily forget your Divinity and the Divinity of all creation.

This is what IT is and IT is neither right nor wrong.

- Awaken.
- All of creation is ONE, Divine and Eternal.
- Forgive yourself. Forgive others. Forgive everything. Remember your Divinity and end your suffering.

Meditation 5

You are, and have always been, an Eternal Divine formless Being.

You are now having an earthly experience in your solid form called a Human Being.

You exist only in the Eternal Now, where cycles of change in energy from the formless to form are the basis of all creation.

You have temporarily forgotten this truth.

Time as you know it is a construct of Ego-Consciousness.

Spiritually speaking, time does not truly exist.

All that exists is the Eternal Now: the past is gone; the future is not here.

Releasing the Ego-Consciousness constructs of time (past and future) means that you and all of creation are Eternal and incapable of ceasing to exist.

Being-Conscious arises only in the Eternal Now - the home of your Divinity. Past and Future are not considerations in the Eternal Now.

- Awaken.
- All of creation is ONE, Divine and Eternal.
- Forgive yourself. Forgive others. Forgive everything. Remember your Divinity and end your suffering.

Meditation 6

You are, and have always been, an Eternal Divine formless Being.

You are now having an earthly experience in your solid form called a Human Being.

You exist only in the Eternal Now, where cycles of change in energy from the formless to form are the basis of all creation.

You have temporarily forgotten this truth.

As a formless Being who has taken solid form in the Eternal Now, your Being expands and contracts with Being-Consciousness and Ego-Consciousness in your mind-made construct of *time* to create what you call *my life*.

That *life* becomes your reality, where you use your free will to engage in relationships in a world which you, as a Divine Eternal Being, have participated in to create as form.

- Awaken.
- All of creation is ONE, Divine and Eternal.
- Forgive yourself. Forgive others. Forgive everything. Remember your Divinity and end your suffering.

Meditation 7

You are, and have always been, an Eternal Divine formless Being.

You are now having an earthly experience in your solid form called a Human Being.

You exist only in the Eternal Now, where cycles of change in energy from the formless to form are the basis of all creation.

You have temporarily forgotten this truth.

There is nothing wrong or right in the Eternal Now. Everything just IS.

- Awaken.
- All of creation is ONE, Divine and Eternal.
- Forgive yourself. Forgive others. Forgive everything. Remember your Divinity and end your suffering.

Meditation 8

You are, and have always been, an Eternal Divine formless Being.

You are now having an earthly experience in your solid form called a Human Being.

You exist only in the Eternal Now, where cycles of change in energy from the formless to form are the basis of all creation.

You have temporarily forgotten this truth.

The past does not exist; the future is not here, right NOW.

The Eternal Now is all that is real.

All experiences and thoughts that you have had, are having, and will have, are steps towards remembering your Divinity within the Divine Source, which is your home.

All your experiences and thoughts, without exception, are opportunities that you may use to restore wholeness (Holiness) and peace within.

- Awaken.
- All of creation is ONE, Divine and Eternal.
- Forgive yourself. Forgive others. Forgive everything. Remember your Divinity and end your suffering.

Meditation 9

You are, and have always been, an Eternal Divine formless Being.

You are now having an earthly experience in your solid form called a Human Being.

You exist only in the Eternal Now, where cycles of change in energy from the formless to form are the basis of all creation.

You have temporarily forgotten this truth.

Ego-Consciousness functions to keep mind-based concepts of past and future *real* in your mind. This affects your access to wholeness and peace.

The workings of Ego-Consciousness and Being-Consciousness are neutral; they are part of your consciousness awakening more and more to its Divinity.

In the Eternal Now, all is in the Divine Right Order.

- Awaken.
- All of creation is ONE, Divine and Eternal.
- Forgive yourself. Forgive others. Forgive everything. Remember your Divinity and end your suffering.

Meditation 10

You are, and have always been, an Eternal Divine formless Being.

You are now having an earthly experience in your solid form called a Human Being.

You exist only in the Eternal Now, where cycles of change in energy from the formless to form are the basis of all creation.

You have temporarily forgotten this truth.

Being-Consciousness is the Eternal Divine consciousness you have that is connected to all of creation; it is unconditional love and it dwells in the Eternal Now.

What you experience as *unconditional love, peace, and wholeness* arises from your encounter with the Eternal Now.

In the Eternal Now, you become truly empowered.

The workings of Ego-Consciousness and Being-Consciousness are neutral, they are part of your consciousness awakening to its Divinity.

- Awaken.
- All of creation is ONE, Divine and Eternal.
- Forgive yourself. Forgive others. Forgive everything. Remember your Divinity and end your suffering.

Meditation 11

You are, and have always been, an Eternal Divine formless Being.

You are now having an earthly experience in your solid form called a Human Being.

You exist only in the Eternal Now, where cycles of change in energy from the formless to form are the basis of all creation.

You have temporarily forgotten this truth.

Spiritually speaking, the world you see is not actually real: it is a construct of your mind. Only you are real as an Eternal Divine Being living in a Human Being form, in the Eternal Now.

You are on a journey to remember your Divinity, using a mental construct called *my life*, one you created using your free will. All of your experiences and thoughts you have created, create now, or will create, have a sacred purpose beyond the understanding of the mundane world.

- Awaken.
- All of creation is ONE, Divine and Eternal.
- Forgive yourself. Forgive others. Forgive everything. Remember your Divinity and end your suffering.

Meditation 12

You are, and have always been, an Eternal Divine formless Being.

You are now having an earthly experience in your solid form called a Human Being.

You exist only in the Eternal Now, where cycles of change in energy from the formless to form are the basis of all creation.

You have temporarily forgotten this truth.

The experiences in what you call *my life* are bridges in consciousness to return you to your Divine Eternal Nature.

Everyone and everything in existence is a spiritual guide for you on your journey, just as you are for others. All are Divine and Eternal.

- Awaken.
- All of creation is ONE, Divine and Eternal.
- Forgive yourself. Forgive others. Forgive everything. Remember your Divinity and end your suffering.

Meditation 13

You are, and have always been, an Eternal Divine formless Being.

You are now having an earthly experience in your solid form called a Human Being.

You exist only in the Eternal Now, where cycles of change in energy from the formless to form are the basis of all creation.

You have temporarily forgotten this truth.

The experiences that you label as *harm* or *loss* are part of a sacred process that you participate in with all of creation to bring you home to your Divinity.

Your *life story* has within it a sacred alchemy, where all persons and circumstances work toward the evolution of your Divine consciousness. Trust this to be true.

- Awaken.
- All of creation is ONE, Divine and Eternal.
- Forgive yourself. Forgive others. Forgive everything. Remember your Divinity and end your suffering.

Meditation 14

You are, and have always been, an Eternal Divine formless Being.

You are now having an earthly experience in your solid form called a Human Being.

You exist only in the Eternal Now, where cycles of change in energy from the formless to form are the basis of all creation.

You have temporarily forgotten this truth.

NONE ARE LOST.

All of creation is sacred and is loved unconditionally by the Source of all Divinity, which you are part of, regardless of how you name it.

There are NO exceptions to this.

- Awaken.
- All of creation is ONE, Divine and Eternal.
- Forgive yourself. Forgive others. Forgive everything. Remember your Divinity and end your suffering.

Meditation 15

You are, and have always been, an Eternal Divine formless Being.

You are now having an earthly experience in your solid form called a Human Being.

You exist only in the Eternal Now, where cycles of change in energy from the formless to form are the basis of all creation.

You have temporarily forgotten this truth.

All of creation is on a journey HOME to the Source of Divinity.

All of creation participates to bring about the collective enlightenment and wholeness of all.

We are all loved unconditionally and are healed into wholeness and serenity, when we remember who we are.

- Awaken.
- All of creation is ONE, Divine and Eternal.
- Forgive yourself. Forgive others. Forgive everything. Remember your Divinity and end your suffering.

Meditation 16

You are, and have always been, an Eternal Divine formless Being.

You are now having an earthly experience in your solid form called a Human Being.

You exist only in the Eternal Now, where cycles of change in energy from the formless to form are the basis of all creation.

You have temporarily forgotten this truth.

Forgiveness is a spiritual practice that brings us back to the truth that all of creation, including thoughts, words, and actions, are forms of energy powering the recollection of the Divinity of ALL.

Forgiveness creates an opportunity for us to enter the Eternal Now.

Forgiveness enables us to experience peace, a wholeness (Holiness) that we share with all of creation.

Even a fleeting awareness of the Eternal Now of our Divinity is powerful enough to begin to transmute pain and loss into wholeness and peace, without exception.

- Awaken.
- All of creation is ONE, Divine and Eternal.
- Forgive yourself. Forgive others. Forgive everything. Remember your Divinity and end your suffering.

Meditation 17

You are, and have always been, an Eternal Divine formless Being.

You are now having an earthly experience in your solid form called a Human Being.

You exist only in the Eternal Now, where cycles of change in energy from the formless to form are the basis of all creation.

You have temporarily forgotten this truth.

Since forgiveness is ultimately a spiritual practice, your *life*, as you experience it, will bring you the precise opportunities you need to experience your Eternal Divine Nature.

- Awaken.
- All of creation is ONE, Divine and Eternal.
- Forgive yourself. Forgive others. Forgive everything. Remember your Divinity and end your suffering.

Meditation 18

You are, and have always been, an Eternal Divine formless Being.

You are now having an earthly experience in your solid form called a Human Being.

You exist only in the Eternal Now, where cycles of change in energy from the formless to form are the basis of all creation.

You have temporarily forgotten this truth.

The most important person to forgive is YOURSELF.

The forgiveness that you give yourself opens you up to your own Divinity. This releases compassion and unconditional love for yourself and for all of creation.

This is how ALL healing is done.

- Awaken.
- All of creation is ONE, Divine and Eternal.
- Forgive yourself. Forgive others. Forgive everything. Remember your Divinity and end your suffering.

Meditation 19

You are, and have always been, an Eternal Divine formless Being.

You are now having an earthly experience in your solid form called a Human Being.

You exist only in the Eternal Now, where cycles of change in energy from the formless to form are the basis of all creation.

You have temporarily forgotten this truth.

Trust in the dance of both your Being-Consciousness and Ego-Consciousness in all of your life experiences to ultimately deliver you to your Divinity in the Eternal Now.

It is in the Eternal Now that you will discover that all is as it IS; you are whole (Holy); and you are never alone, because you are at One with all of creation.

- Awaken.
- All of creation is ONE, Divine and Eternal.
- Forgive yourself. Forgive others. Forgive everything. Remember your Divinity and end your suffering.

Meditation 20

You are, and have always been, an Eternal Divine formless Being.

You are now having an earthly experience in your solid form called a Human Being.

You exist only in the Eternal Now, where cycles of change in energy from the formless to form are the basis of all creation.

You have temporarily forgotten this truth.

Fearlessly, trust your unity with the Divine and all of creation to present opportunities in your life for you to recall your Holiness (wholeness).

You will be guided to that knowing by both your Being-Consciousness and Ego-Consciousness.

- Awaken.
- All of creation is ONE, Divine and Eternal.
- Forgive yourself. Forgive others. Forgive everything. Remember your Divinity and end your suffering.

Meditation 21

You are, and have always been, an Eternal Divine formless Being.

You are now having an earthly experience in your solid form called a Human Being.

You exist only in the Eternal Now, where cycles of change in energy from the formless to form are the basis of all creation.

You have temporarily forgotten this truth.

As you remember that you are a Divine Eternal Being who participates in creating this world and all the experiences in it as your *life story*, you will increasingly come to know and experience the Eternal Now.

And ultimately, this sacred paradox will unfold within you; the Eternal Now renders forgiveness unnecessary, because *All* are loved, *All* are without judgement, and *All* cannot cease to exist. None are lost.

Creation rejoices in you as itself.

Experiencing Unconditional Love

Forgiveness lifts the veil to unconditional, eternal love.

Forgiveness is a gateway to remembering our Divinity and is the only knowing that leads us to truly experience unconditional love.

In our knowing of who and what we are as Eternal Divine Beings, we are more deeply connected to the Source of all of creation, or to the Higher Power of Our Understanding, here, we sense our true purpose and our unity with all of creation.

Knowing this connection, we can recognize that condemnation and judgement of ourselves, others, and life are not useful, this differs from our use of judgement or discernment for decision making on a mundane level in our day-to-day lives.

This form of detachment is an inherent experience in Being-Consciousness. Our Ego-Consciousness fades as we enter the Eternal Now, in which powerful knowledge can enter into our consciousness.

In our Being-Consciousness, we become the Observer, observing life. We see a larger picture of life and embrace the idea that there may be mysteries beneath those which we see on the surface: mysteries that hold untold possibilities.

Every possibility realized is an expression of the Divine. When we accept this fact, we can love unconditionally. How we respond to that expression is entirely personal.

Part Four

Forgiveness As A Spiritual Practice

Forgiveness is a spiritual practice in which our *life story* is the path to remembering who we truly are: Divine Eternal Beings.

Anything and anyone who appears in our life story can become a gift to deepen our forgiveness practice, no matter what their role.

Ego-Consciousness will also judge others and remind us of past harms. This creates opportunities that we can use to bridge to our Being-Consciousness and bring about our profound awakening to our Divinity in the Eternal Now. Anticipate this but be gentle and forgiving with yourself first.

Some will discover their own way along this path, others may struggle with indecision or the lack of trust within themselves and may need guidance to enable them to take that first step, and beyond. Those that wish for a starting point and a route to follow, can use these five steps:

1. Acknowledge the pain and disappointment you are experiencing.
2. Breathe in a mindful way.
3. Forgive yourself for expecting *what was* to be different from *what it was*, or *what is* to be different from *what it is*.
4. Forgive yourself for expecting others for not being who you wished them to be or for being different to who they are.
5. Remember who and what you truly are.

Once you have discovered your path, let it develop, change it to lead you in whatever direction you need it to go, own it, become part of it as it becomes part of you.

Wholeness and Holiness

Holiness is wholeness of spirit. Our forgiveness walks take us to a greater awareness of what and who we are as spiritual beings - Divine Eternal Beings enabling us to encounter our Wholeness/Holiness.

- No matter what form your physical body takes, spiritually, you are still whole.
- No matter what you do or don't do with your life, spiritually, you are still whole.
- No mind-made or man-made idea, practice, or thing can take away your Wholeness/ Holiness: It is hardwired into the Real You.

This truth is meaningful because without it, you will fear the death of the body. Ego-Consciousness makes this fear ever-present in our minds, but through greater awareness of our Being-Consciousness we think of forgiving, or actually forgive, and here, we grow in the peace of our eternal nature, in the Eternal Now.

Breath and Spirit

Our breath is the *in-spirit* or *In Spirit-ation* of our spirit form. Each time we breathe a relaxed breath, we take ourselves closer into Being-Consciousness and move more deeply into the Eternal Now, into our spiritual form.

Try doing relaxed breaths in times of stress, pain, anxiety, or fear. (The relaxed breath is a breath that moves the abdomen out rather than the chest and the shoulders up.)

I say to my clients, "Drop you belly, let it fall out as you breathe in." For most of us, this is difficult, because we fear the look of an outward abdomen and instinctively hold our abdomen in with tension. But the very power of physical/spiritual interface lies right in this maneuver of *dropping your belly*. Ancient Yogis knew this and shared this with the world.

It is no coincidence that relaxed deep breathing helps to alleviate pain, anxiety, and tension in the body, and improves alertness in the present moment. It is my belief that we manifested ourselves this way in co-creation, to have a mechanism by which we can move, at will, in and out of our Being- and Ego-Consciousness through use of our breath.

The times in our lives when we suffer physical and mental pain, knowing our existence as a Divine Eternal Being can help us to transcend fear and pain, as we breathe into our spirit form. Consider the power of your breath in a new light: it can bring you closer to peace and wholeness.

The Spirit is Tangible

Is Spirit tangible? It may well be. The electromagnetic field in and around the body is measurable and can be influenced by acupuncture, and other energy therapies, and may be a part of what we call spirit, or, at the very least, evidence of our form being beyond the physical.

The aura is often seen and depicted in illustrations of revered Beings as a golden or white glow around the figure. Many people today, myself included, have the ability to see auras around people and in nature. I have been able to see a soft light emanating from my fingers and toes since I began my work in bioenergetics in 1997. I am NOT alone in this; we all have this ability, it's just a matter of activating it. And trust me when I say it shocked me when I first saw it.

I believe that this electromagnetic field that so many of us can see is part of our connection to the Divine. Since we do not live in lead boxes, this field must be constantly in us, radiating through us, and extending into the universe. I know it to be the connection that we all have to all of creation and, ultimately, to the Source of all creation.

PART FIVE

Reflections For Forgiveness As A Spiritual Practice

~ For confusion about who we are

I am a Divine Eternal Being having an earthly experience.

I am inseparable from All of creation and its Source.

The Eternal Now is where my Divinity dwells.

As a Divine Eternal Being, I choose to leave the Eternal Now to forget my Divinity so that I may return to it.

As a Divine Eternal Being, I know that in the Eternal Now, all is in the Divine Right Order.

Awareness of the Eternal Now is all I need to consciously embrace my Divinity.

My Divinity is constant, whether I am aware of it or not.

~ For consideration about forgiving

Forgiveness creates a timeless gateway for me to remember my Divinity.

I forgive until I am established in the truth that I am a Divine Eternal Being.

I forgive because it heals me by returning me to my Divine self.

When I know that All are Divine, I will no longer need to be afraid of loss and I can then forgive with ease.

I am no longer afraid of ceasing to exist. I will forgive with ease and later I will realize that no forgiveness is necessary, because I am forever whole (Holy), as is all of creation.

I may create suffering for myself and others, because I have forgotten my Divinity.

Others may have created suffering for themselves and others, because they have forgotten their Divinity.

All of creation has a sacred purpose in my life story to restore me to my Divinity.

~ For confusion about the meaning of one's life

As a Divine Eternal Being, I have created my life with the co-operation of all of creation.

As a Divine Eternal Being, I see all events of my life as opportunities to expand my consciousness.

As a Divine Eternal Being, I know that I have created my life and its stories as part of my spiritual journey home.

As a Divine Eternal Being, I know that in the Eternal Now, all is in the Divine Right Order.

As a Divine Eternal Being, I know that all of creation co-operates with my thoughts to create the life that I am currently experiencing.

As a Divine Eternal Being, I know that I co-operate with all of creation to create the life that I am experiencing.

All experiences that I have in my life story are opportunities to remember that I am a Divine and Eternal Being.

I have free will and can choose whether I wish to remember that I am a Divine Eternal Being.

~ For anxiety and fears of death

I am a Divine Eternal Being, so I can never cease to exist.

My form is of a dynamic eternal energy and changes all the time, never ceasing to exist.

I need never fear the transformation of my form, because I will never cease to exist.

When I transform, my form as energy returns to the formless Source of all forms.

All that is real is this moment, and all in this moment is what is.

I am part of the Source or Higher Power of My Understanding, nothing can change this.

Nothing created can be lost, because all of creation is one, never ceasing to exist.

I am a perpetually changing form of eternal energy.

I will transform again and again, because energy is never lost; it only changes form.

Matter and energy are one. Form and formless are one. My-self and God are one.

I can never truly be alone, because I am part of all creation, timeless and eternal.

I am loved, because all of creation rejoices in me as co-creator with all of creation.

All is well in this present moment, because I am at one with all of creation.

~ Questions for reflection about forgiveness of oneself

Do I really know who and what I am?

Am I able to consider forgiving myself?

Am I willing to forgive myself?

Does forgiving myself feel right for me? If not, why? If yes, Why?

I ask myself, lovingly and with compassion and forgiveness, how I would feel if I released any guilt, shame and self-loathing that I have toward myself?

If I were free of so much of the guilt, shame and self-loathing that I carry, what would take its place?

I ask myself, lovingly and with compassion and forgiveness, if I hide or project my guilt, shame and self-loathing onto others or situations without even knowing it?

If I have hidden or projected my suffering unconsciously onto others, can I remember who and what I truly am and forgive myself?

How would my life be if I were to release the pain and suffering that I experience towards a person or situation?

I ask myself, lovingly and with compassion and forgiveness, if it is possible that there may be a connection between what

I am feeling or experiencing today in my body, mind and spirit and my forgiveness walk?

~ Questions for reflection about forgiving others

Am I stuck in an old mental pattern about someone that has limited ME?

Is it possible for me to consider that those who have harmed me are also Divine Eternal Beings who know that the consequences of their behaviours were real, harmful to me and/or others, and are accountable to the laws of my group, community or society?

Is it possible for me to consider that those who have harmed me have forgotten their Divinity and acted in accordance with forgetting their Divinity, their accountability not withstanding?

Is it possible that there is a mystery to all things in creation for which I am a part of, but not entirely aware of?

Is it possible for me to consider that the people and situations in my life are, in some mysterious way, part of the life story that I have created for myself for some sacred purpose, as far-fetched and even painful as that may seem to me right now?

Is it possible that I have yet to see the way in which the harm done to me or others, whom I cherish, has a sacred purpose beyond what I currently understand?

Is it possible for me to trust a Higher Power of My Understanding to continue to move with my connection to it to reveal deeper meaning to me?

Is it ok for me to be right where I am with forgiveness, with no expectation and no guilt or shame?

Can I consider that, no matter what I do or do not do about forgiveness in my life, I am and will always be a Divine Eternal Being connected, inseparably, to the Higher Power of My Understanding as a loved creation?

Part Six

Where To Go From Here: Taking A Forgiveness Walk

Begin your Forgiveness Walk, *not* your Forgiveness Work.

I hesitate to use the phrase Forgiveness Work, because forgiveness is not work, it is a walk along a spiritual path, a journey that leads you home, and to who you truly are.

You may be wondering where to go from here. After using the meditations and reflections suggested in this book (in whatever way works for you), the first thing that I can recommend, is to become familiar, if you have not already done so, with a method to experience the Eternal Now or the present moment in your life.

Don't be afraid. Such an experience does not necessitate you undergoing hypnosis; it does not mean you will need to be put in a trance; this is an experience that we already have, but one which we have not yet singled out in our awareness. An example of entering the Eternal Now is when you are in any situation in which you are fully and singularly focused on one task or thing and have no sense of time passing, when everything is peaceful and, seemingly, going in slow motion.

In finding my way to the Eternal Now, the words of Eckhart Tolle have greatly inspired me: he speaks of how he draws from a variety of ancient traditions to bring sacred wisdom to the present day. Tolle's book, *The Power of Now*, is iconic in that regard. In this, he guides you patiently and gently into an exploration of the Eternal Now, or the *present moment*, as he often refers to it.

There are numerous other authors who also speak to entering into the *now* that you can research online: as a starting point, refer to *Works That Inspired "A Course in Forgiveness"* in Part Nine.

But be clear, entering into the Eternal Now is not a prerequisite to forgiving, you will be led into the Eternal Now and, thus, access your Divinity by just choosing to consider forgiving, because forgiveness is a bridge to the Eternal Now.

Find ways to see the Divinity in yourself, others, pets, and nature by watching life. Once you begin to look for Divinity, you will see it. The greatest challenge is to see the Divinity in what you resist: it may be difficult to do this, but it is there, and you will see it if you try.

You may try placing the word *Divine* before everything that you observe or experience. Yes, everything. Divine

Tasma; Divine food; Divine water; Divine air; Divine tree; Divine whale; Divine moss; and so on. In this way, you may begin to sense the essential Divinity in all of creation.

Some may choose to create and join groups to discuss forgiveness in which clear guidelines are set to create emotional safety for the whole group. For example, pointing out that details of harm are not permitted, but rather simply referred to as *Harm*, so the focus remains on the Forgiveness Walk vs. the harm.

Create a Forgiveness Policy for your own life first and then consider creating one for the environments that you live in: family, groups, schools, communities, organizations. A workplace forgiveness policy could be a powerful tool too, to prevent and address the harmful outcomes of any workplace horizontal violence and physical violence.

Find a group to actually take a Forgiveness Walk with together, perhaps for a cause or goal that you wish to bring peace or hope to. If you fundraise as well, consider whether there is a forgiveness policy in the organization that you wish to donate to.

Consider becoming an ambassador of a local or national Forgiveness Day.

If you are creative in any way, use forgiveness as a theme in the Arts with public exhibits for the same.

For sports and other social events, dedicate the game to family, community and global forgiveness.

The helping professionals, other trained safe persons, and Twelve-Step programs are powerful supports to any Forgiveness Walk.

You may wish to start a private journal in which you record your own reflections about where you are at with forgiving yourself and/or others.

And always know that, even if your Forgiveness Walk is just standing still this is fine too, because as you experience stillness, you remain on your journey to the Eternal Now and your own Divinity.

> *"Three things in human life are important:*
> *The first is to be kind; the second is to be kind;*
> *the third is to be kind."*
>
> Henry James

Part Seven

Epilogue

I dream of a world where, one day, we no longer need forgiveness to enable us to see the Divinity in all of creation: it will happen innately and instinctively.

In order for us to reach that destination, forgiveness is needed to change the world, one forgiving gesture at a time. Each act of forgiveness elevates all consciousness to a new vibration.

Forgiveness is For Giving - For giving awareness of the Divine that exists in all situations and in all of Creation.

Part Eight

Addendum

The Story that Inspired this Book: One of my Forgiveness Walks

"Mom, dad is dying."

I could not believe what I heard at first, but the look on my son's, Sebastian's, face said it all.

I had seen my ex-husband, Leslie, about eight-months before: he looked so thin that I spontaneously cried when he came to the door to get Sebastian (who was 21 at the time).

"What's wrong; what has happened to you; you look so thin and pale?" I asked through my tears. He calmly reassured me that it was just some complications of dental surgery that caused him to have difficulty eating. I was not convinced. I came into the house and Sebastian asked me what was wrong, why was I crying. I said, "Your dad is very, very sick; something is very wrong."

We had been divorced for 10 years by this point, and he was married again. He and Sebastian had recently found their way to a deeper relationship as father and son.

After hearing Sebastian say, "Mom, dad is dying," I felt shocked and frozen. I softly said, "Son, your dad has a spouse; I can't interfere." But Sebastian persisted and said, "Mom, he needs help, please help him, dad is dying, he is starving to death."

When I reflect on my response, I know that this happened: I went into the Eternal Now. Sebastian, my sense of time, the room, even my sense of me, fell away. There was complete stillness.

I then said from the stillness, "It's ok son, I will help your dad." I went straight to my kitchen and started cooking. Nothing, not one idea or memory of the past, what went wrong for us, nor what was said or done, mattered.

Leslie has celiac disease and with it a neurological disorder that weakens his lower body, but not his mind. When Sebastian asked for help for his father, it was because he knew that his father could not use his body to make food, or even open packages to prepare food for himself.

I went about cooking his favourite foods that I could remember, and I pureed them because Sebastian said that Leslie was having difficulty swallowing.

I labeled the dishes and Sebastian took them to Leslie's office and home. Given what I feared would be the repercussions, I thought it took a lot of guts to take food to his father's home, but nothing was going to stop our son from helping his father, nothing and no-one.

We eventually assisted Leslie to move to a new apartment and I went back and forth after work between his apartment and my home, with my dear friend Elma's help, once a week for a year, caring, cooking and cleaning for him. During this time, I never felt anything but a drive to care for him and for my son: there was just no room for anything else.

Gradually, he gained strength and began to put on weight. He would weep with gratefulness and I wept with him, for the joy of seeing him heal. One year later, divorced from his wife, he moved into my home and we are remarried.

If anyone had ever told me that I would remarry my first husband, I would have thought it unlikely. We were very fortunate to have had a calm and respectful divorce that focused on our son's needs.

I will always remember going to the bank and saying a silent, "thank you" to Leslie for his financial support of both Sebastian and myself while we were divorced. I never took for granted what his hard work was doing for the quality of Sebastian's and my life.

I would tell friends about what was happening, they would be shocked, and many would weep because they were so moved by what they called, "An incredible love story; a true story of forgiveness; a miracle."

It was their responses that showed me the power of what I was, "just doing." I never took the time to acknowledge anything that either he or I were doing as *forgiveness*. We just knew that he was dying, and that experience took us into the Eternal Now almost every time we were together.

Today, we recall and celebrate the miracle of our lives together again. We know now that we never had all the answers the first time around, we still don't. We are forgiving again and again the expectations we have of each other and supporting each other to be just who we are. We put each other first.

Our family healed when Leslie got sick. We all share a deeper relationship with each other and an appreciation of the time we have together. Our lives have been forever changed by the gifts we received through forgiveness.

PART NINE

Works That Inspired
A Course in Forgiveness

Beyond my own life experience, the following were, in one way or another, inspirations for this book. There are countless of other resources that speak to the Eternal Now, consciousness, forgiveness, time, energetic healing and non-duality, but these sources listed touched me deeply.

- ADAM (2008). Intention Heals.
- Alan W. Watts (philosopher, writer, and speaker), various audio recordings.
- Amit Goswami (1995). The Self-Aware Universe: How Consciousness Creates the Material World.
- Anodea Judith (2004). Eastern Body, Western Mind: Psychology and The Chakra System as a Path to the Self.
- Barbara Ann Brennan (1988). Hands of Light: A Guide to Healing through the Human Energy Field.
- Barbara Ann Brennan (1993). Light Emerging: The Journey of Personal Healing.

- Brian Greene (2010). The Elegant Universe: Superstrings Hidden Dimensions and the Quest for the Ultimate.
- Candace B. Pert (1999). Molecules of Emotion.
- Coleman Barks (1997). The Essential Rumi
- Dean Radin (2006). Entangled Minds: Extrasensory Experiences in a Quantum Reality.
- Deepak Chopra (1990). Quantum Healing: Exploring the Frontiers of Mind Body Medicine.
- Deepak Chopra (2001). Perfect Health: The Complete Mind Body Guide.
- Dolores Krieger (1996). Therapeutic Touch, Inner Workbook.
- Eben Alexander M.D (2017). Living in a Mindful Universe. A Neurosurgeon's Journey into the Heart of Consciousness.
- Eben Alexander M.D. (2012). Proof of Heaven. A Neurosugeon's Journey into the Afterlife.
- Eckhart Tolle (2004). The Power 0f Now: A Guide to Spiritual Enlightenment.
- Eckhart Tolle (2008). A New Earth: Awakening to your Life's Purpose.
- Eckhart Tolle (2009). Oneness with all of Life: Inspirational Selections from a New Earth.
- Eknath Easwaran (2007). The Bhagavad Gita.
- Fritjof Capra (2010). The Tao of Physics: An Exploration of the Parallels between Modern Physics and Eastern Mysticism.
- Gary Zukav (2007). The Seat of the Soul.
- Gary Zukav (2009). The Dancing Wu Li Masters.
- Helen Schucman (1976). A Course in Miracles.

- Herman Hesse (1981). Siddhartha,
- Idries Shah (1991). The Way of the Sufi.
- Jill Bolte Taylor (2009). My Stroke of Insight.
- Joachim-Ernst Berendt (1991). The World is Sound: Nada Brahma: Music and the Landscape of Consciousness.
- John Briggs & F. David Peat (1999). Seven Life Lessons of Chaos: Spiritual Wisdom form the Science of Change.
- Jon Mundy (2012). Living a Course in Miracles: An Essential Guide to the Classic Text.
- Louise Hay (1984). You Can Heal Your Life.
- Lucinda Vardey (1995). God in All Worlds: An Anthology of Contemporary Spiritual Writing.
- Michael Williams (2012). One: The Gospel According to Mike.
- Peter H. Fraser and Harry Massey, with Joan Parisi Wilcox (2008). Decoding the Human Body-Field. The New Science of Information as Medicine.
- Paulo Coelho (2006). The Alchemist.
- Rainer Viehweger (2011). Understanding the Universe through Global Scaling: Looking at the World with Fresh Eyes.
- Richard Gerber (2001). Vibrational Medicine, The #1 Handbook of Subtle-Energy Therapies.
- Shafica Karagulla & Dora van Gelder Kunz (1989). The Chakras and the Human Energy Fields.
- Stephen Mitchell (1999). Tao Te Ching.
- What the Bleep Do We Know? It's time to get wise! Film. (2004). Samuel Goldwyn Films.

As a final note, I would like, again, to wish you peace and love: hold onto these lessons within *A Course in Forgiveness* and take them with you always; find your Divinity; end your suffering; remember who You Truly Are.

Ramona "Bobbi" Stobbart-Kasza

> *"It is so mysterious to me how all the work that I have done regarding my own growth, and with couples and individuals in mind, body and soul, has taught me that, ultimately, forgiveness creates trust, and with that trust there can be a personal sense of divine love within and, thus, in all of life."*
>
> *…Bobbi*

Ramona "Bobbi" Stobbart-Kasza is an Eternal Divine Being who has roles as a spouse, a mother, an author, and a health professional, for 39 years. Living in Alberta, Canada, her interests are in exploring consciousness, the natural world, singing, playing the piano, gardening, and creative movement.

Since 1996, Bobbi has dedicated her life to helping people through her work as a spiritual and bioenergetic healer. She uses an energy model in creative arts, journal writing, and other modalities to support wholeness and peace in those with whom she works. This book arises from Bobbi's experiences in which forgiveness and non-duality are the focus.

Please visit <u>acourseinforgiveness.com</u> to learn more about A Course in Forgiveness and how to experience a life with unconditional love, wholeness, freedom, and peace.

Manufactured by Amazon.ca
Bolton, ON